Snow Cones in Heaven

Written by Sara Conover McKinnis
Illustrated by Caragh Buxton

www.motsdemerebooks.com

She and Mom were ready for bed,
Just settling down, when sweet Hannah said:

"What will it be like when you and me,
Go live with Jesus, and when will that be?"

Mom didn't think twice before she replied,
"It will be nice!" But Hannah just sighed.

Hannah looked up as if she could see,
What Heaven was like and how it would be.

To Mom's surprise, little eyes filled with tears,
And she whispered so low, with something like fear:

"I don't want to go and be by myself...with no books
to read and nobody else.

I'm afraid I'll be lonely and sad, don't you see?
Why can't we stay home, just you and me?"

Mom thought, "What have I done that Heaven seems so bleak?" She said a small prayer, then started to speak.

"Oh sweet Girl, no mind can know and no eye has seen, The wonderful place that Heaven must be.

Let me see if I can tell in your terms,
Of our home with Jesus that faith affirms.

First of all, you'll not be alone,
We'll all be together there at God's throne.

Old friends and new wait for us there,
And everyone will have stories to share!

We'll get there when angels come give us a ride,
No matter what they will always be by our sides.

Whether on ponies, in boats or hot-air balloons,
We will ride to Heaven, not a moment too soon.

In the mornings, it's breakfast with those we love,
And then it's time to go feed the doves.

We'll play our games and go for walks,
We will read and sing, and enjoy our talks.

Trees that are angels grow in the park.
If you stumble and fall, it won't leave a mark.

Jesus stays with us, and He laughs and plays.
He loves all his children and with us spends His days.

Under that sun, we'll have so much fun!
Snow cones to eat and races to run.

Then in the cool of the afternoon air,
We'll want to thank God, so we'll say a prayer.

We'll settle down and take a great nap;
Where could be better than in Jesus's lap?

All of this to say, there is nothing to fear.
Heaven may be a little bit like here.

A bit like here, but with much more that's good.
Just imagine a while longer if you could.

No one feels bad and hearts are all gladness,
And there is never, ever a reason for sadness.

Hannah was still, then nodded and stared.
And after a moment, her dimples flared.

"I get it now, and I think it's OK,
If we all live there together someday.

But tomorrow, I want to go to the park,
Then read books and hear the dogs bark."

Mom laughed and said, "You have a deal.
Now a kiss for you - sweet dreams to seal!"

"I like Heaven, Mommy, it's shiny and free -
I'll go to sleep now and dream you there with me."

Just a Few of God's MANY Promises!

Matthew 19:14 - Jesus said, "Let the little children come to me, and do not hinder them, for the kingdom of heaven belongs to such as these."

John 14:2-4 - ²My Father's house has many rooms; if that were not so, would I have told you that I am going there to prepare a place for you? ³And if I go and prepare a place for you, I will come back and take you to be with me that you also may be where I am. ⁴You know the way to the place where I am going.

1 Corinthians 2:9 - "What no eye has seen, what no ear has heard, and what no human mind has conceived"- the things God has prepared for those who love him.

Meet the Author

Sara Conover McKinnis is an Oklahoma native who has melded her passions for storytelling, history, and spirituality into meaningful works for kids and caring adults of all ages. Sara has penned spiritual, patriotic, and community-centric pieces to enrich the lives and key understandings for her own children, as well as children and families of every community.

She resides upon the beautiful plains of Oklahoma (most of the time) and in the fabulous Colorado Rockies (as often as she is able) with her husband and their children. In addition to being a super-mom and weaving creative narratives, Sara enjoys exploring other diversions such as American politics, French language studies, archaeological shipwreck diving, and British mystery novels.

Sara wishes to express profound and humble gratitude to Jesus Christ for leading her on such a rich journey. To Him be the glory for amazing adventures (and for all of the adventures still to come).

Learn more by visiting **www.motsdemerebooks.com**

www.ingramcontent.com/pod-product-compliance
Lightning Source LLC
Chambersburg PA
CBHW061751290426
44108CB00028B/2965